SNOW SEARCH DOGS

by Maida Silverman

Consultant: Wilma Melville, Founder
National Disaster Search Dog Foundation

New York, New York

Special thanks to Wilma Melville who founded the:
National Disaster Search Dog Foundation
206 N. Signal Street, Suite R
Ojai, CA 93023
(888) 4K9-HERO
www.SearchDogFoundation.org

The Search Dog Foundation is a not-for-profit organization that rescues dogs, gives them professional training, and partners them with firefighters to find people buried alive in disasters. They produce the most highly trained search dogs in the nation.

Special thanks to CARDA
(Canadian Avalanche Rescue Dog Association)
in British Columbia
www.carda.bc.ca

Design and production by Dawn Beard Creative and Octavo Design and Production, Inc.

Credits

Cover, Front (left), Patrick Cone Photography, (top right), Canadian Avalanche Rescue Dog Association, (center right), (bottom right), AP / Wide World Photos; Back, (top), Canadian Avalanche Rescue Dog Association, (center), (bottom), AP / Wide World Photos. Title page, Patrick Cone Photography. Page 3, Masha Nordbye / Bruce Coleman Inc.; 4-5, Matt Hage / Alaska Stock; 6, Bob Winsett / Index Stock; 7 (both), Robin Siggers, Fernie Alpine Resort; 8-9, Tom Evans / Alaska Stock; 9, 10 (inset), AP / Wide World Photos; 10-11, Jeff Schultz / Alaska Stock; 12-13, Ralph Reinhold / Animals Animals / Earth Scenes; 13, Mary Evans Picture Library; 14-15, AP / Wide World Photos; 15, Canadian Avalanche Rescue Dog Association; 16-17, Jenny Hager / The Image Works; 17, Canadian Avalanche Rescue Dog Association; 18-19, 20-21, Bill Becher; 22, Christian Racich / Alaska Stock; 23 (both), Peter Bardhhle / Vidicom-TV; 24, AP / Wide World Photos; 24-25, AP / Wide World Photos; 26-27, Calvin W. Hall / Alaska Stock; 27, Masha Nordbye / Bruce Coleman Inc.; 29(top), (center left), Photodisc / Fotosearch; 29(center right), Photospin.com; 29(bottom left), (bottom right), Photodisc / Fotosearch.

Library of Congress Cataloging-in-Publication Data

Silverman, Maida.
  Snow search dogs / by Maida Silverman ; consultant, Wilma Melville.
    p. cm. — (Dog heroes)
  Includes bibliographical references (p.   ) and index.
  ISBN 1-59716-017-2 (lib. bdg.)   ISBN 1-59716-040-7 (pbk.)
  1. Search dogs—Juvenile literature. 2. Rescue dogs—Juvenile literature.
  3. Snow—Juvenile literature. I. Melville, Wilma. II. Title. III. Series.

  SF428.73.S55 2005
  636.7'0886—dc22

                              2004020753

For more information, write to Bearport Publishing Company, Inc., 101 Fifth Avenue, Suite 6R, New York, New York 10003. Printed in the United States of America.

1 2 3 4 5 6 7 8 9 10

Table of Contents

Trapped!

Ryan was skiing down a steep mountain **slope**. Suddenly, a huge wall of snow came rushing down the mountain toward him. It was an **avalanche**! The snow swept Ryan up and carried him along.

An avalanche in Alaska

About a million avalanches occur each year around the world. Most do little damage because they happen where there are no people or houses.

When the wild ride stopped, Ryan was buried. He pushed his hand up to break through the snow, but he couldn't. He was trapped. There was only a tiny pocket of air around him. Ryan tried to breathe slowly and stay calm.

To the Rescue

Rescuers rushed to the avalanche site. They quickly began to search the area for **survivors**. Some rescuers, like Keno, were dogs. They knew just what to do.

Keno first ran back and forth with his nose in the air. He was sniffing the **scent** coming up from the ground.

A Colorado rescue team

Suddenly, Keno stopped. There was something under the snow. He barked and began to dig.

Soon, the dog saw Ryan's hand. Robin, Keno's **handler**, and the other rescuers ran over. They helped dig Ryan out. The lucky skier had been buried for 30 minutes. He was almost out of air.

Keno and his handler, Robin Siggers

Keno was the first dog in Canada to save the life of someone buried in an avalanche.

7

Avalanche

Many tons of snow race down a mountain during an avalanche. No one can **outrun** it. No wonder an avalanche is called "white death."

The moving snow kills some people right away. Other people die when they are thrown against rocks or trees.

Sometimes, a person is buried alive under the snow. A person's body heat and breath turn the nearby snow into a thin coat of ice. Air can't get in.

If not found quickly, the person will die from a lack of air. Using snow search dogs is the fastest way to find people buried in avalanches.

Allen Weaver and his snow search dog Zephyr practice digging for a person buried in the snow

More than 500 people died in avalanches in the United States between 1950 and 2003.

No Time to Lose

Snow search dogs also find people who get caught in **snowstorms**. Hikers and skiers may become lost or hurt when heavy snow falls. Trained search dogs are often the only way to find these people before it's too late.

Rescue workers and a snow search dog look for people after an avalanche in Austria.

All people have a scent that dogs can smell. After an avalanche, dogs can quickly crisscross large areas of land as they sniff for a human scent. It would take people, who look for things with their eyes, much longer to search the same area.

Mountain climbers in a winter storm

A dog's nose is 1,000 times better at smelling than a person's nose.

The First Snow Search Dogs

Saint Bernards have been saving lives for centuries. More than 300 years ago, many of these dogs lived at a **shelter** for people traveling in the mountains of Switzerland, a country in Europe. Barry was the shelter's most famous snow search dog.

A Saint Bernard

One day, Barry and a man were walking when they saw an avalanche. The man rushed back to the shelter, but Barry refused to go. He then did something he had never done before. He ran away. Later that night, Barry showed up dragging a little boy. Barry had found the child near an icy **cliff**.

A 1921 illustration of a Saint Bernard rescuing a man buried in snow.

Barry saved more than 40 people during his lifetime.

Snow Dogs Today

In the 1930s, the army in Switzerland began training dogs. They taught the animals to search for people buried in avalanches. Since then, training snow search dogs has spread to many parts of the world.

Today, helicopters and ski lifts often bring snow search dogs high up into the mountains where they are needed. Saint Bernards, however, are huge. They are harder to carry than smaller dogs. Now, most snow search dogs are smaller and lighter than Saint Bernards.

A Saint Bernard can weigh as much as 200 pounds.

Tucker and his handler (the man in the yellow vest) practice at an avalanche training camp in Utah.

Choosing a Pup

Many handlers begin training their dogs as puppies. The pups that will make the best rescuers love to hunt for things. Trainers use the pup's love of hunting to help him or her learn to search for buried humans.

Hasty, a snow search dog, plays in the snow.

Dogs from many **breeds** now help in snow rescues. These animals need a thick coat to keep them warm in the cold weather. They need to be strong enough to climb **rugged** mountains with ease.

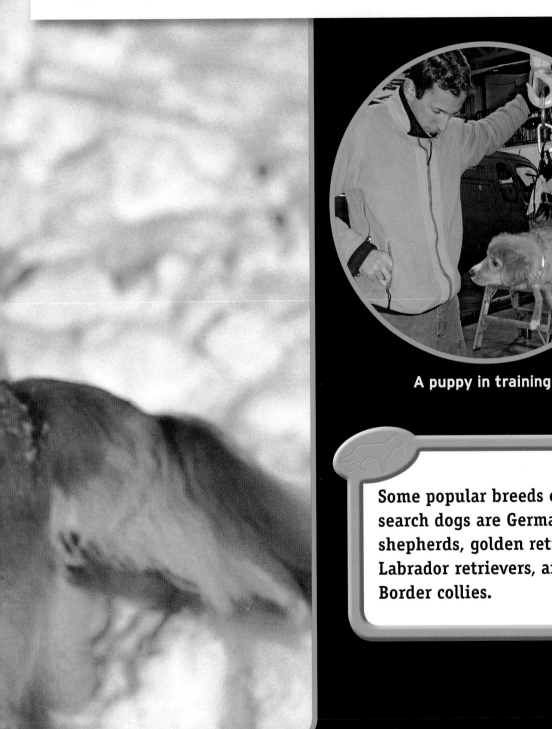

A puppy in training

Some popular breeds of snow search dogs are German shepherds, golden retrievers, Labrador retrievers, and Border collies.

Simple Searches

Training starts simply. While a person holds the dog, the handler runs away and jumps into a **shallow** pit. Then the dog is let go. When he finds his handler, he's rewarded with playtime. Finding people is fun!

SEARCH DOG

The game gets harder over time. The handler is covered with snow to teach the animal that people can be buried out of sight. Then the handler is buried deeper in snow and farther away to make him harder to find. Every time the dog finds the person, he gets to play.

Helicopters sometimes lower a snow dog into a search site. The animal must learn to stay calm while hanging from a rope.

Hard Searches

Bill is a **trainer**. He's pretending he was caught in an avalanche. He's buried under three feet of snow with a sealed bag of doggie treats. Bill lies still and tries to stay calm. It's scary to be buried!

Colorado has more avalanche deaths than any other U.S. state. Most Colorado avalanches occur from December to April.

A snow search dog named Ursa is digging above Bill's head. Suddenly, Bill sees a paw and then a nose. Ursa keeps digging until Bill is free. Bill rewards her with the doggie treats. Ursa barks happily. She has been training for two years. Ursa is now ready for a real rescue.

Ursa in action

A Real Mountain Rescue

Andy was snowboarding high in the mountains of Europe when an avalanche covered him with snow. He lay buried for 20 hours. Andy thought he was going to die.

A snowboarder in mid-air on Mt. Ogden, Alaska.

A snow search dog can smell a person buried under as much as 35 feet of snow. A person's scent, however, must travel up for the dog to find it.

If it were not for a dog named Falk, the searchers might have stopped looking for Andy. Falk started barking when he found a spot where human scent was rising from the snow. He alerted his handlers and then began digging. Rescuers soon brought shovels and broke through to Andy. He was alive.

Rescue workers examine Andy for injuries.

Falk and his handler

Danger on the Job

Snow rescue is dangerous for **victims** and rescuers. One of the biggest dangers is that a second avalanche might happen. Sometimes the smallest movement can start the snow moving again.

An Alaskan team after an avalanche search and rescue in 2001

A handler and a snow search dog look for missing people after an avalanche in Russia.

Often the countryside where the dogs and handlers search is dangerous. They climb over steep, rugged ground. A dog might cut his foot on a hidden rock or fall into a hole in the snow. Handlers won't let their dogs search if they think an area is too dangerous.

Some of the most dangerous avalanches occur in places with few trees.

Happy Dogs

People love the snow. Every year, more and more people go skiing, snowmobiling, and snowboarding in the white **wilderness**. Danger, however, often comes along with the fun.

Some people who play in the mountains now carry special beepers. If they are caught in an avalanche the beepers can help others find them.

Some skiers now wear backpacks with air bags. If an avalanche occurs, the air bag inflates, helping the person stay on top of the snow.

Snow search dogs are the ones who most often find people buried in snow. These dogs don't ask for much as a reward for their **heroic** work. Some dogs beg for a tasty treat, while others just want a game of fetch or tug-of-war.

Snow dog and handler play tug.

Snowmobilers are more likely to be caught in avalanches than people who take part in other winter sports.

Just the Facts

- Avalanches can rush down a mountain at 185 miles per hour.

- A snow search dog named Doc saved the life of a skier who was buried in an avalanche. The man was so happy that he had a picture of Doc tattooed on his chest.

- German shepherds make the best snow search dogs because they are very strong. They also don't get tired and the cold doesn't bother them. They can even sleep in the snow.

- If a person gets caught in an avalanche, she should move her arms and legs as if she's swimming. This action may stop her from sinking into the snow.

- Sometimes people buried under snow can't tell which way is up. The easiest way to find out is to spit. The spit will always move down.

- Some states, such as Colorado and Utah, have avalanche information centers. Radio stations broadcast the centers' forecasts every morning. These forecasts list the areas where avalanches are likely to occur.

Common Breeds: SNOW SEARCH DOGS

Saint Bernard

Border collie

golden retriever

German shepherd

Labrador retriever

avalanche (AV-uh-lanch) a large amount of snow, ice, or earth that suddenly moves down a mountain

breeds (BREEDZ) types of a certain animal

cliff (KLIF) a high, steep rock

handler (HAND-lur) someone who trains and works with an animal

heroic (hi-ROH-ik) very brave and courageous

outrun (out-RUHN) to run faster, farther, or longer than someone or something

rescuers (RESS-kyoo-urz) people or animals who save someone who is in danger

rugged (RUHG-id) rough and uneven; jagged

scent (SENT) the smell of an animal or person

shallow (SHAL-oh) not deep

shelter (SHEL-tur) a place where you can stay safe

slope (SLOHP) ground that is not flat and forms a slant

snowstorms (SNOH-*stormz*) storms with strong winds and heavy snow

survivors (sur-VYE-vurz) people who live through a disaster

trainer (TRAYN-ur) someone who teaches a person or animal how to do something

victims (VIK-tuhmz) people who are hurt, injured, or killed by a person or event

wilderness (WIL-dur-niss) an area with thick forests where few people live

Bibliography

Gorrell, Gina K. *Working Like a Dog: The Story of Working Dogs Through History.* Toronto, Canada: Tundra Books (2003).

Singer, Marilyn. *A Dog's Gotta Do What a Dog's Gotta Do.* New York, NY: Henry Holt (2000).

Read More

Haggerty, Edward C. *Working Dogs.* Danbury, CT: Grolier Educational (1997).

Jennings, Terry. *Landslides and Avalanches.* Mankato, MN: Thameside Press (1999).

Silverstein, Alvin, and Virginia Silverstein. *Different Dogs.* Brookfield, CT: Twenty-First Century Books (2000).

Spilsbury, Louise, and Richard Spilsbury. *Crushing Avalanches.* Chicago, IL: Heinemann Library (2003).

Tracqui, Valeria. *Fact to Face with the Dog: Loyal Companion.* Watertown, MA: Charlesbridge Press (2002).

Learn More Online

Visit these Web sites to learn more about snow search dogs and avalanches:

www.avalanche.org

www.comdens.com/SAR

www.svguide.com/w01/w01avalanche.htm

www.vidicom-tv.com/avalanche_angels

Index

About the Author

Maida Silverman has been involved with children's books for many years. She has been a book designer as well as an author. She lives in New York.